Conquering Your Flesh

Gregory Dickow

Conquering Your Flesh

Printed in the United States of America

For information, please write
Gregory Dickow Ministries,
P.O. Box 7000
Chicago, IL 60680

or visit us online at www.changinglives.org.

Table of Contents

Conquering Your Flesh

Introduction

A prosperous man learns the art of conquering himself.

God has an inheritance for you! He wants you to experience it. He wants you to enjoy the fullness of life and peace.

Christians should become the most successful people in the world. We should become the kindest people in the world. We should become the most powerful people in the world. But it will not come just because we're saved. It's going to come through conquering ourselves. Victory and success are found in the conquering of your flesh.

A man who conquers himself,

cannot be conquered.

A man who controls himself cannot be controlled. It is our unconquered flesh, and our unconquered attitudes that defeat us and keep us where we are at.

Would you like to know your calling? Your calling is found in your conquering. You will discover your calling based on how much flesh you conquer. It's in the overcoming of a thing that we prepare for our promotion in life. Whatever you conquer in your life, will point to your calling.

What is the thing we have to conquer or overcome? It is our flesh. You don't need to overcome the devil. The devil has been thrown down. The devil has been defeated. He has been stripped. He has no power over you.

It is our flesh that we have to defeat. And it's not as hard as we may think.

Ephesians 1:3 says, *"Blessed be the God and Father of our Lord Jesus Christ who hath blessed us."* That's translated as "has already." It says, "He has already blessed us with all spiritual blessings in heavenly places in Christ."

All blessing begins in the spirit, not the flesh! Notice He says they are "spiritual blessings." That means they are in spiritual places or "in the spirit."

If all of God's intended blessings are "in the spirit," then we need to "get in the spirit" to receive them. Just as if all His intended blessings were in your backyard, you would need to get in the backyard to receive them!

The problem is, Galatians 5:17 says, *"The flesh opposes the spirit..."* Since our blessings are "in the spirit," then the flesh opposes our blessings. Since that is the case, it is vital that we clarify what the flesh really is. Too many Christians are trying to overcome their flesh, but they don't really understand what it is. As Paul said, they are *"boxing without aim, as beating the air"* (1 Corinthians 9:26).

As we define the flesh and the spirit, we will understand how to yield to the spirit instead of the flesh.

Again, this is so important because when you walk in the spirit, then you will experience the blessings that God already has for you—because they're in the spirit. It's our flesh trying to keep us from them.

Conquering the flesh won't be as hard as you think. It's not going to take a forty-day fast. You're thinking, "Glory to God!" Enjoying food is not the flesh—eating too much is the flesh, but enjoying to eat is not. Having an ice cream cone isn't the flesh. The last time I had an ice-cream cone, if I'm not mistaken, the Lord was enjoying it with me! That's how I know that having an ice-cream cone is not of the flesh!

I know of times in my life, where I have been more in the flesh, while fasting, than I was while feasting. This may come as a shock to some, but we need to get our thinking straight on this subject. (This is not to say that fasting is wrong).

Before we go on, let me encourage you not to be condemned if you have failed as a believer, or in some areas of your life. Perhaps you're reading this book because you are struggling.

In Matthew 26:36-41, Jesus was about to go to the cross. He took some of His disciples to pray and He said in verse 36, *"'Sit here while I go pray.'* He took Peter and the sons of Zebedee and began to be sorrowful and very heavy."

The Lord is so merciful. He took Peter, who was about to deny Him. A few chapters earlier, Jesus referred to Peter as the devil! This shows how merciful God will be with us. He forgave Peter, restored him, and took him back. Think about it—you have never been called the devil, but He called Peter the devil and He still took him back. You haven't had it that bad, so realize, if He took Peter back, He will always take you back, even when you have blown it. That's how good God is!

In verse 38, Jesus said, "'My soul is exceedingly sorrowful even unto death. Tarry here and watch with me.' He went a little farther and fell on His face and prayed and said, 'Oh my Father if it's possible let this cup pass from me; nevertheless, not as I will but as you will.' And he comes unto His disciples and finds them asleep and says to Peter, 'what, could you not watch with me one hour? *Watch and pray that you do not enter into temptation. **The spirit is indeed willing but the flesh is weak.'"***

If the devil was our biggest problem Jesus would have said, "The spirit is willing but the devil is strong," or, "the spirit is willing but the devil is your problem." But, He didn't say that the devil was the problem. He said the ***flesh*** was the problem.

The devil has been defeated. When Jesus died for your sins and rose from the dead He conquered the devil. In case you were not fully aware—when Jesus died on the cross, He went down and He spoiled the principalities of darkness and He made a public display of them (Colossians 2:13-15). He literally had the devil by the throat and He was dragging him around through hell so that all the demons could see that their lord and their master, the devil, had been defeated. He took the keys of hell and death and He gave them to us, and now we have authority in this life (Revelation 1:18, Matthew 28:18). So it is not the devil—it is our flesh we must conquer.

In Ephesians 1:3 we saw that all blessing begins in the spirit. Again, all inheritance begins in the spirit. The enemy of our inheritance is not the devil. The enemy of our inheritance is the flesh. Galatians 5:17 says, *"The flesh opposes the spirit and the spirit opposes the flesh."* So if the flesh opposes the spirit, the flesh also opposes our blessing—our inheritance. If you're not experiencing the fullness of your inheritance, it's because you're in the flesh, or you are walking by the flesh and its dictates. Let's change that . . .

Part I

A Fresh Look At the Flesh vs. the Spirit

The Flesh Profits Nothing

Chapter One

John 6:63 says, *"It is the Spirit that (quickens) gives life. The flesh profits nothing."*

The flesh profits nothing. I don't know about you, but if something profits nothing, I don't want to keep doing it. If it's bringing "zero" profit, I am not interested!

Why do people walk in the flesh? It's not because they have to. Christians don't walk in the flesh because they are bound to the flesh. They've been redeemed. We're born again. We're new creatures. We're spirit beings. Most people walk in the flesh because we think it will accomplish something. We think it will produce something. Why do we get angry? We think that by being angry, it will get someone to do something. If I get angry with you, I could possibly motivate you to do something different that what you were doing—but in the end, it won't bring any profit. Anger is an emotional reaction that comes from thinking it will bring profit to us, which leads to an outburst of our flesh. It profits nothing, the Bible says. The flesh profits nothing (John 6:63).

Now, before looking more closely at what the flesh is or how it takes shape, let's look at what the spirit is. Again, in verse 63, Jesus says, *"The Words that I speak unto you, they are spirit and they are life."* So He's telling us here, what it means to walk in the spirit.

Walking in the spirit means walking in the Word of God. When you're walking in the Word, you're walking in the spirit—simple as that.

Now, the actual definition for the word "spirit "is: that part of our being that is conscious of what's above us.

In fact, allow me to give you three definitions—of the spirit, the soul and the flesh. The spirit is: that part of our being that is conscious of what's ***above*** us. Our soul is that part of our being that is conscious of what's ***around*** us. And our flesh is that part of our being that is conscious of what's ***in*** us. The flesh is ***NOT*** our body.

A fuller definition of the "flesh" is more clearly explained in the next chapter.

The part of us that can look above us, being conscious of what's ***above*** us, is our spirit. What is above us? Heaven is above us. "Blessing" is above us. Remember, all blessing begins in heavenly places, in spiritual places. The Bible says in Colossians 3:1, *"Keep seeking the things that are **above** where Christ is seated, at the right hand of God."* Our mind needs to be on the things that are above us, not on the things that are around us, not the things that are going on the inside of us. Now in Galatians 5:16, Paul says, *"This I say then, walk in the spirit and you shall not fulfill the lust of the flesh. For the flesh lusts against the spirit, and the spirit against the flesh. And these are contrary the one to the other, so you do not do the things that you would."*

Notice what Paul says, *'the flesh lusts against the spirit,'* or the flesh is at war against the spirit. The spirit is at war against the flesh. And these are contrary to one another so that you do not do the things that you desire. The flesh is fighting the spirit, and the spirit is fighting the flesh, so that you cannot do the things that you wish, or have the things that you want. The war between your spirit and your flesh is the thing that is preventing you from having the things that you wish. It's keeping you from having the things that you desire, or from having the things that God wants you to have. And so we must crucify the flesh. The Bible doesn't say, "Battle with the flesh day and night." The Bible says, "Crucify your flesh." That's a one-time death. Now, yes, I understand the Bible says to take up your cross daily because that flesh is always trying to resurrect itself. But the first step is to crucify it once and for all—not to live in a constant battle with your flesh.

Now, the only way to effectively crucify the flesh is to identify and to reduce the flesh to its simplest definition. Then it's easy to deal with. Too many are confused about what it is (and hopefully, I am not adding to that confusion). "Am I in the flesh because I am overweight?" "Is my flesh just wanting to eat another piece of pie? "Is my flesh this? Is my flesh that?" Let's answer this . . .

Two Mindsets

Chapter Two

The flesh, in its simplest definition, is the opposite of the spirit. We found out in John 6:63 that walking in the spirit means walking in the Word of God. Therefore, walking "in the flesh" means walking in what is contrary to the Word of God. And it starts with our thinking. Let me make this as clear as I can: The flesh is not our body. The flesh is not the devil.

The flesh is a way of thinking!

Someone may say, "Oh, I stumbled and fell. Does that mean I was in the flesh?" "I sinned. Does that mean I was in the flesh?" "I blew it. Does that mean I was in the flesh?"

Brace yourself for this answer: No—not necessarily. Let me explain it to you this way: Being "in the flesh" caused you to sin; being "in the flesh" caused you to blow it. But "blowing it" is not being "in the flesh."

Being "in the flesh" is different than just falling, making a mistake, sinning, or blowing it. Being in the flesh is not an action. Being in the flesh is ***a way of thinking.***

The flesh is a way of thinking that leads to a bad decision, which is where failure comes from. Failure doesn't come from being "in the flesh." Failure doesn't come from being out of control in your emotions. Failure comes from making bad decisions and bad decisions come from being in the flesh. Bad decisions come from being emotionally ruled rather than ruling over your emotions.

The flesh is a way of thinking, a system of thought. It's a way of thinking that opposes the Word of God and opposes righteousness. Oh, read this closely, now. The flesh stays alive through a system of thought; therefore the flesh is crucified by taking thoughts captive.

Romans 8:4, says, *"that the righteousness of the law might be fulfilled in us, who walk not after the flesh but after the spirit."*

So "righteousness" is fulfilled, not by the flesh but by the spirit. *"For they that are after the flesh do mind the things of the flesh"* (Romans 8:5).

Notice what Paul says here: *"They that are according to the flesh set their minds on the things of the flesh. But they that are according to the spirit, the things of the spirit. For the* ***mind set*** *on the flesh is death" (Romans 8:5-6).* What he is saying is: ***the flesh is a "mindset"***.

The flesh is a system of thought—not a system of behavior. It's a way of thinking that opposes the Word of God. Since Jesus said, "My Words are spirit", then any words that are contrary to the Bible, (contrary to Jesus), are the flesh. The flesh is a way of thinking that eventually will lead us to corresponding actions or decisions. For example, the flesh is a way of thinking that ***leads*** to over-eating; a way of thinking that ***leads*** to illicit sex; a way of thinking that ***leads*** to immorality; a way of thinking that ***leads*** to anger.

It's the root cause of these behaviors. In Galatians chapter 5 Paul talks about the "works of the flesh" including lasciviousness (which is simply the word for "having no borders, no boundaries in your life, no restraints in your life"), immorality, idolatry, witchcraft, factions, etc. These are the manifestations of a wrong way of thinking.

Let me give you an example of what the flesh is—a young lady, who is lonely, thinks that by being with a man, she is going to feel loved and accepted—she is in the flesh because of her way of thinking. And it is that way of thinking that leads her to sin. The flesh is given breath and life through a wrong way of thinking.

Misconceptions of the Flesh

Chapter Three

Here is another example of how the flesh thinks—I bet you never would've thought this is the flesh: someone says, "Boy, that sin that I just committed, that's just going to ruin me. That's just going to finish me. God cannot be happy with me right now." That may sound humble and God-fearing, but it is "the flesh" because it is contrary to what the Word says! The Word says, "As far as east is from west, so far has He removed your transgressions from you." When you say, "Oh, man, I don't know if I can overcome this sickness, or this financial problem,"—that's the flesh.

See, we have thought that the flesh is: being mean, being evil, being lustful, over-eating, etc. We think all those things are the flesh, when in fact, those are merely the manifestations of wrong thinking.

How about this one: "If I just pray enough I know I'm going to get the answer to what I need!" That is the flesh. The Spirit says, "I have the answer." The flesh says, "If I just fast enough, I'm going to be able to crucify my flesh."

I'm not saying you shouldn't fast, but fasting won't change the way you think. Fasting will help to get your mind to better focus on spiritual things and will help discipline your body. But it doesn't change the way you think. You need the Word for that. See, your flesh has an appetite, and it is fed by thoughts and patterns of thought, not food. While our body needs to be disciplined, our flesh needs to be starved and crucified!

When you say, “I don’t know if I can make it through this situation,” that is the flesh. How do we know it’s the flesh? We know because it opposes the spirit. The spirit says, “I can do all things through Christ, which strengthens me” (Philippians 4:13).

Now think about this: the flesh cannot believe the Word. The flesh is a wrong belief system, and must be crucified. The flesh can only believe what it sees.

In Romans 8:8, Paul says, *“So they that are in the flesh cannot please God.”* Why? Because the flesh can’t have faith, and without faith, you cannot please God. Now we are getting to the root of the flesh.

The flesh is the opposite of faith. “Faith” is activated by hearing the Word of God. “Flesh” is activated by hearing something contrary to the Word of God. All fear is, is listening to your flesh. All depression is, is listening to your flesh.

This should empower you to now identify what the flesh is, and crucify it—it is a mindset that is contrary to the Word of God. But let's get more specific.

Part II

Simple Steps To Crucifying The Flesh

Crucify your flesh!

But how?

Let me give you some simple steps...

Walk in the Spirit

Chapter Four

In one sense, our flesh is already crucified, as Galatians 5:24 says, *"They that are in Christ Jesus have already crucified the flesh, with its passions and desires."*

So by being ***IN CHRIST,*** our flesh is crucified. What we are really dealing with is: conquering the flesh's tendencies to try to control and dictate our thought life, which in fact, really controls the outcome of our lives. There is though, something to be said about being ***IN CHRIST.***

Those who know who they are "in Christ" have crucified the flesh. Those who walk in His righteousness have crucified the flesh. It's righteousness that comes from God versus righteousness that comes from our flesh. As we think "righteousness," as we know we are righteous through the blood of Jesus and we flood our minds with this righteousness—this causes the flesh to stay dead.

Let's go on to see how to further crucify our flesh.

Walk in the Spirit. Galatians 5:16 says, *"Walk in the spirit, and you will not fulfill the lust of the flesh."* So if we want to crucify the flesh—or not fulfill the lust of the flesh, it says we need to walk in the spirit.

What does it mean to walk in the spirit? We know that walking in the spirit is walking in the Word, or being Word-minded.

Walking in the spirit is not as hard as we have made it out to be. It's not as hard as the devil would love for you to think it is. It's easy to walk in the spirit because the Holy Spirit lives in our spirit. The devil wants you to think that walking in the spirit is only for an elite few. That it's only for the Green Berets of Christianity—only they can walk in the spirit. No, walking in the spirit is for everybody. Let me put it to you this way: you don't have to be "spiritual" to walk in the spirit.

Walking in the spirit is what makes you "spiritual". By walking in the spirit you are immediately being "spiritual."

You are not spiritual because you had a dream. You are not spiritual because you had a vision. You are not spiritual because you know a couple of Scriptures. You are not spiritual because you have been saved twenty or thirty years. You are not spiritual because you know all the latest news in Christianity.

What makes you spiritual is following the direction and the leading of your spirit and the Holy Spirit. And you follow the leading of your spirit very easily, very simply.

You may say, "What do you mean, 'this is easy?' I've tried so hard to stop doing this sin. I've tried so hard to stop acting this way. I've tried so hard to stop having this bad attitude."

Attitude simply reflects a way of thinking. A behavior simply reflects a way of thinking. So if we can deal with our way of thinking, then we will fix our attitudes and our behaviors.

Be Aware of the Conflict

Chapter Five

In Galatians 5:17, Paul sets up the battlefield when he says, "The flesh is against the spirit and the spirit is against the flesh." Since the Scripture says, "Walk in the spirit, and you will not fulfill the desires of the flesh," our focus should be on the spirit, not the flesh. (The "spirit" carries a dual meaning as it sometimes refers to our spirit and sometimes to the Holy Spirit.—The fact is, they are often interchangeable because the Holy Spirit resides in our spirit.) So let's see how to practically walk in the spirit—this will enable us to conquer our flesh.

You have to be aware of the conflict. It's one thing to be in a battle. It's altogether another thing to be in a battle and not know where the attack is coming from. Did you know that you are in a battle every day of your life? You are in a fight every day of your life. Do you know what the fight is for? You are made up of three parts. You are a spirit, you have a soul and you live in a body. The problem with your body is that your body carries the desires of the flesh in it. You always should talk care of your body but you should never take care of your flesh, and there is a difference between those two things.

So you have to understand there is a battle. Your spirit and your flesh are vying for the control of your soul and your body. Your spirit and your flesh are fighting for control. Oh yes, the spirit fights! Your spirit is a fighter. "The violent take the kingdom by force." He is talking about our spirit. There is a warrior inside every one of us, and you are more than a conqueror. You can win this battle. I'm going to show you how easy it is to win this battle. But you must embrace the reality that you are in a battle for the control of your soul—your thought-life.

Be aware. Be knowledgeable. Don't be a Christian ostrich who sticks his head in the sand and says the battle isn't there. Our battle is not with other nations. Our battle is not with the economy. Our battle is not with the devil. Our battle is with our flesh. If you can learn to walk in the spirit, God will take care of protecting you. God will take care of providing for you and He will take care of empowering you. So there is nothing to worry about. What's going on in the world will not control the outcome of your life when you know how to walk in the spirit.

Put First Things First

Chapter Six

The next step to crucifying your flesh is you must put first things first. What do I mean by that? As we already read in Galatians 5:16, *"Now I say then, walk in the Spirit and you shall not fulfill the lust of the flesh."* You must put first things first. "Walking in the spirit," is an example of putting first things first.

Imagine this: We are sitting in the dark with absolutely no light. So we bind the devil, and the spirit of darkness, in Jesus' name. We decide to have a prayer meeting to get rid of the dark. The prayer meeting doesn't work, so how about if we fast? Maybe we need to shout, "darkness leave!" Maybe we need to march around the darkness seven times, but when will we know we did a full circle, since we can't see anything?

Darkness leaves when we turn on the lights! If we followed this experiment, would darkness leave because we prayed enough? Would darkness leave because we fasted enough? Would darkness leave because we shouted enough? Would darkness leave because we started a prayer meeting? When would darkness leave? It would leave when the lights came on. The light comes and the darkness leaves. When you walk in the spirit, the flesh is overpowered. When you speak the Word, the light goes on. Psalm 119:130 declares, *"the entrance of His Word brings light."* Walking in the spirit is like turning the light on.

What does he say in Galatians 5:16? *"Walk in the Spirit and you shall not fulfill the lust of the flesh."* He doesn't say "overcome your flesh and then you will be able to walk in spirit," (which is how most Christians try to live their life.) They try to overcome their flesh so that they can then qualify for walking in the spirit, and God doesn't say it works that way. It actually works the exact opposite. *As* you walk in the spirit, you will not fulfill the desires of the flesh. So the emphasis needs to be on walking in the spirit, not on trying to beat up your flesh.

The more of God's Spirit that we walk in, the less the flesh will influence our lives, our decisions, and our will. Religion teaches us that as we stop sinning then the Holy Spirit will come and empower us. But it is the exact opposite; it is our union with the Holy Spirit that overpowers the works of the flesh just like light overpowers darkness.

Darkness does not overpower light. Light overpowers darkness. Most Christians think they have to conduct spiritual exercises to overcome the flesh. It's not the exercises that you do that will conquer the flesh. It is as you walk in the Spirit. And what is the Spirit? The Spirit is the Word. The Spirit and the Word are one. And the Word is light.

All our striving to make the darkness leave could not make it leave, could it? All of your striving to make your flesh obey you is not going to make it obey you. Your flesh hates you. Your flesh hates God, so believe me, it hates you. What has to happen? Light has to come. The Bible says the entrance of His Word brings light.

Walking in the spirit means two things:

A. It means walking in the Word or yielding yourself to God's way of thinking.

B. Walking in the spirit means walking in love. When you walk in love, the spirit overpowers the flesh and the demands it is placing upon your life.

Your flesh is constantly placing a demand upon your life; but when you walk in the Word, and you walk in love, the flesh is overpowered.

As soon as the light comes, the darkness leaves. As soon as you are walking in the spirit, your flesh is out-matched. Walk in the spirit and you shall not fulfill the lust of the flesh. You walk in the spirit and then the flesh is starved. When anything starves, it eventually dies.

I realize some of us are having slower deaths than others in our flesh! "Oh Pastor, the death of my flesh is such a slow death. Is there any quick pill I can give it or any quick shot I can give it?" No, because it resides in your thinking. What you have to do, is overtake it with a system of thinking and a way of thinking that causes you to yield to God's Spirit. As a result, you will not fulfill the lust of the flesh.

As soon as somebody says, "Don't think of a pink elephant right now!" What happens? You think about a pink elephant.

What does that prove? It proves that when you try to stop a habit by focusing on it, you will often become frustrated.

Let me give you another example. James 4:6-8 says, *"God resists the proud but gives grace to the humble. Submit yourselves therefore to God, resist the devil and he will flee from you."*

The key to the devil fleeing from you is not in you resisting the devil first. First, you are to submit to God.

God and his Spirit are one. God and His Word are one. As you submit to God and to His Word, then you release the power to resist the devil. Then he must flee.

James goes on to say in verse 8, *"Draw near to God and He will draw near to you. Cleanse your hands and purify your hearts."* Notice—first he says, "draw near"—then "cleanse your hands." First we must draw near. He doesn't say "cleanse your hands and purify your hearts; and then you qualify to draw near." Yet, most Christians think they have to get sin out of their life so that God will accept them.

God accepts you right now because of Jesus' blood. God loves you right now. God says "Draw near to Me." God puts first things first, and so should we.

You Are Not Alone

Chapter Seven

The next step to conquering your flesh is to realize you are not alone, I am not saying "Hey, let's all stay in the flesh since there are so many others in the flesh." What I am saying is: you are not alone in the battle. Many have faced it before you, including Paul, the apostle.

Look at Romans 7: 21-23. *"I find this law at work: when I want to do good, evil is right there with me. For in my inner being, I delight in God's law... but I see another law waging war* ***in my mind*** *and making me a prisoner of the law of sin at work within my members"* (NIV).

Notice what He is saying: "even when I want to do good, evil is waging war against my mind, trying to get me to obey the law of sin." This is the flesh! Even the great apostle had to deal with it. So don't be surprised you are experiencing this in your life. You feel this battle in your members—you feel these feelings, thoughts and images coming to you—and you may think, "I guess I am not really saved." That's what the devil wants you to think, "I am not really saved," or "I am not really spiritual." Do you know that the most spiritual people in the world still have to deal with their flesh? They still have a flesh that is warring against their spirit. That is why it's not about how spiritual we are. It's not about how much knowledge we have. It's about walking in the Spirit. It's walking in the Word. It's speaking the Word; meditating on the Word; getting our minds absorbed in the Word of God to the point where it causes us to overtake the flesh.

You say, “Well, when do you get to that point?” You start right now! And don’t be condemned that you have struggled. Don’t be condemned that you have fallen. A righteous man may fall but he gets up! God’s Spirit lives in you. You are not alone.

The great apostle, Paul, dealt with his flesh. He faced this battle and won. You are not alone. You have a great cloud of witnesses surrounding you. Don’t let the devil trick you into thinking that you are the only one that struggles with these things. And don’t let him trick you into thinking you can’t make it. You can and you will!

Feed and Honor Your Spirit

Chapter Eight

Recognize that your flesh is not the real you anymore. 2 Corinthians 5:17 says, *"If any man be in Christ He is a new creature, the old things are passed away and all things have become new."* Your flesh isn't you anymore. You are a spirit. If you have been born-again, you are a new creation. You are not connected to your past. Your past has been cut off, divided from you. Honor the new you.

You have a new spirit. You have been given a new love. You have a new Father. You are connected to a new covenant. You have a new name. You have a new family, and you have a new way of thinking. Honor the "new" in you!

As we feed and honor the new man in us, our spirit, we starve the old man. We honor the new man in us by feeding the new man in us, by putting the Word in our mind and in our heart, and changing the way we think. Sometimes people don't want to read the Bible because they feel condemned when they read it.

When the Word condemns you, you are reading it in the flesh, not in the spirit. God never condemns. Romans 8:1 says, *"There is therefore now no condemnation for those who are in Christ Jesus; who walk not after the flesh, but after the spirit."*

How do I read the Bible "in the spirit", where this verse is concerned? You say, "I am in Christ Jesus. I am a new creature in Christ; therefore I am not condemned."

You see, he also says, "*For those who do not walk according to the flesh*, but according to the spirit." Remember, the flesh is a way of thinking. I am in the flesh when I base my condemnation or my righteousness, on what I do or how I act. I am in the spirit when I realize, "I am forgiven because of Jesus; not because of my good or bad works." Do you see the different mindsets here? That is the difference between the flesh and the spirit. The flesh says, "I'm condemned because of what I did." The spirit says, "I'm forgiven in spite of what I did." It is that simple. Follow what your spirit says and you will have, therefore, "no condemnation." As your thinking changes in examples like these, your behavior will change as well!

Part III

Seeing in the Spirit

Things That Limit Us From Seeing God's Perspective

Chapter Nine

So walking in the spirit means walking in the Word, but let me give you another definition of the word "spirit."

The spirit is man's "vertical window." Remember, horizontal is side by side, while vertical is up and down. Therefore the "spirit" is man's vertical window giving him the ability to see and think like God. The vertical window is to see from a vertical point of view. It is to see from God's perspective—to see a situation from God's point of view.

Your “horizontal window” gives you the ability to see only what is in front of you. The vertical window is the ability to see above you, from God’s vantage point. He sees higher than we see, and when we see what He sees and think as He thinks, we will do as He does. You are never going to be able to do what He does until you first see what He sees.

What are some of the things that limit us or hinder us from seeing things God’s way?

1. Our Current Circumstances. If we let them, our current circumstances will limit us. It may be a doctor’s report, or your empty wallet. Perhaps your wife is mad at you or your children aren’t serving the Lord. Your current circumstance may include some symptoms in your body that aren’t good, that aren’t healthy. Perhaps you are without a husband or without a job...or both!

Regardless, your current circumstances are trying to limit what you can see. The flesh is: to be limited in what we can see. The flesh is: to only see what our eye can see, to only hear what our ear can hear.

God says to you, "I am going to get you into a life of healing, a life of blessing, a life of prosperity." You say, "But God, I can't see it; I can't understand how it is going to happen." When you say that, you are in the flesh. You may say, "But I love the Lord. How can I be in the flesh?" Again, it's a way of thinking. When you say, "Well, I know God says that we are healed by His stripes but I don't see how it's going to happen," you are in the flesh. The fact that you don't see how it is going to happen is limiting your ability to believe it *is* going to happen. Stop worrying about whether you can figure out how it is going to happen.

There are a lot of things that I believe God wants to do in my life, that I don't know how they are going to happen. That is not going to stop me. If it does stop me from believing, then I am in the flesh. But if I say, "It doesn't matter that I don't understand how it is going to happen. I know that God's Word said: He started it, and He is going to finish it in my life," then, I am in the spirit. I am in the spirit because I am not limited by what I see.

Someone said, "No, you are really in the spirit when you are experiencing spiritual things and when you are experiencing visions and dreams and healings and miracles; that's when you are in the spirit." That's not true. You are in spirit when what you see is not limiting you; and what you hear is not limiting you. That is when you are in the spirit. You could have a vision, you could have a dream, you could have a miracle and still be in the flesh, because you are being limited by what you see.

In other words, I might feel healthy right now, I might feel well right now; but I don't declare that I am healed because I feel well right now. I declare that I am healed because God's Word says I am healed. That puts me in the spirit. You see, we mistakenly think that the manifestation of something is the proof that we believe something. But I don't need to wait for my miracle to show up before I believe that I have received. So, to walk in the spirit means, I believe that I have received even when the miracle hasn't shown up yet.

Let's say the miracle shows up and all of the sudden I am rejoicing. If I am only rejoicing because the miracle has shown up, I am in the flesh. If I only can get excited and I only rejoice when I see the manifestation, I am in the flesh. Get in the spirit. That means the Word is now—regardless of what it looks like right now.

The flesh says, "I'll have it when I see it. I'll believe it when I see it. I'll know its mine when I see it." The spirit says, "I don't need to see it to know that I have it."

Now, if you stay "in the spirit," it is eventually going to manifest. That's walking in the spirit. So, our current circumstance is the first thing that can limit us from seeing things God's way.

2. Our Previous Experience. What has happened in your past must not limit you. You are in the flesh when you say, "Well, my record shows..." or "This has always been the farthest I can go..." Wait a minute! Doesn't the Bible say, "If any man be in Christ he is a new creature. The old things are passed away, and all things are become new"? Forget about what the record shows. Stop thinking, "This is the limit of how far I can go. This is the limit of how much money I can make. This is my ceiling." You are in the flesh when you have "ceilings." There is no ceiling with God. There is no salary cap with the Lord. God says, "Look, I can do exceeding abundantly beyond all that you can ask or think." So start asking and start thinking in the spirit rather than in the flesh!

Don't allow yourself, your dreams, or the thing you are believing for, to be limited by your current circumstance or by your previous experience.

"Well it seems like every year about this time, sickness comes into our house." That's your previous experience. That was last year—it doesn't have to be this year. This is a new year, this is a new day, and this is the day that the Lord has made. Rejoice and be glad in it! His steadfast mercy and loving kindness are new every morning and his faithfulness never comes to an end! (Psalm 118:24; Lamentations 3:22).

That's how you have to look at it. Your previous experience is not the dictator of your future. It can be, but we are not going to allow it to be in our lives anymore. You say, "Well, I talked to that person and I tried to sell our product and I tried to sell our company's services to that client but they already rejected me in the past." Forget about the past! Maybe this time they will accept you. Maybe this time they'll want it. What's it going to hurt?

Take the limits off! Previous experiences can be very negative, because everyone has had bad experiences in the past. If we replay the images of our past experiences, they will limit us from the future blessing God wants to bring into our lives. Previous experiences will limit our ability to walk in the spirit and see things God's way.

3. Other People's Experiences. "Well son, I've been around," someone may say. "I've seen a lot, and I would say, based on my experience you can only go so far." "Based on my experience, young lady you really just don't have what it takes." Your attitude needs to be, "Take your experience and go bury it somewhere, because I don't really care about what you have experienced. Don't try to put some sort of bondage on me. Your experience might have put you in some bondage, but it's not going to put me in bondage!"

You may think a person is experienced in a particular subject, but experience must not be our god! I am not saying to ignore practical knowledge like gravity. If someone said, "Based on my experience, every time someone jumps off this third story roof they break their leg," you should listen!

Don't say, "Well, I'm in the spirit. I can do it." If you do, you are going to break your leg, because that truth isn't based on that man's experience. *That* truth is based on a law called "gravity," which is irrespective of somebody's experience.

Someone, however, may say, "I have an aunt who died of that. She started coughing like you are coughing. It sounded just like that. In fact yours sounds worse." That's somebody's experience. Now you are walking in the flesh if you begin to think it could happen to you because it happened to Aunt Sue!

When you establish their experience as your expectation, you are in the flesh. You may think you are being humble. You may think you are just being true to your heart and you're going to be humble and respect what that person said. That is the flesh, because their experience is now limiting what God can do in your life.

4. People's Words. The fourth thing that will hinder us from seeing things God's way is people's words—ours and others'. The words that we speak over our children can make or break their future. We must be careful to always speak positive words, words of confidence, words of faith and words that take the limits off of them rather than put words on them that will hinder their ability to be great.

Don't ever say to your kids, "Well, based on what I have seen and the way you do your homework, you are never going to make it to a really good college. You might as well just get ready for community college and get a job and do this and do that." I am not saying there is anything wrong with community college. I am simply saying don't ever put limitations on others.

If my children want to go to Harvard, they can go to Harvard. If they want to go to Yale, they can go to Yale. If they want to go to the community college, that might be O.K. too. The point is, I am not going to allow my words to limit them.

Don't allow other people's words or failures to limit you. They may say, "Well I tried that once." Maybe that was the problem: they only tried it once. You might have someone say to you, "I tried to start a business like you are, and it doesn't work." Don't let them bring their bad track record into your record. ***It might be the picture of their past, but it is does not have to be the prophecy for your future!***

You must guard your heart. Words will try to put all sorts of limitations on you. Some people don't want you to succeed because it may make them feel even worse that you made it, and they didn't. You ought to go back to them and say, "If I can make it, you can make it. Why did you quit after two or three tries?" If Thomas Edison would have been like that, then we all would still be in the dark right now. He didn't invent the light bulb until after he had tried hundreds and thousands of experiments.

Concluding Thoughts

Chapter Ten

Freedom is found in conquering your flesh. A man who conquers himself cannot be conquered. It's your unconquered flesh and your unconquered attitudes that defeat you. It's not the devil that defeats you—not others, not your circumstances.

Your calling is found in your conquering. It's in the overcoming of a thing that we prepare for our promotion in life.

You see, we are not only in the flesh because we act like the devil, or because we act like a fool. We are in the flesh when we are unwilling to adapt to God's way of thinking and God's way of looking at things.

You say "I'm kind of old now and you can't teach an old dog new tricks." Where is that in the Bible? First of all, you are not a dog, and secondly your youth is renewed like an eagle, so you don't have any excuse not to learn new tricks. We don't learn new tricks anyway. We learn God's way of thinking. We're not learning gimmicks or tricks.

Go to Isaiah 46:10: *"I am God... declaring the end from the beginning and from ancient times the things that are not yet done saying 'My counsel shall stand.'"* Remember, God sees the end from the beginning. The flesh loves to stay safe. This is the flesh keeping us from God's unlimited view and God's unlimited vision for our lives.

I'm telling you right now, start looking up. When God told Abraham, "You are going to have a son and he is going to have sons after him and your descendants are going to be like the stars of heaven and the sands that are by the seashore and I am going to make you a father of a multitude of nations," Abraham could not see it, based on what he was looking at. So the Bible says God took him outside (Genesis 15:5), so He could get him out from under his ceiling. God said, "Look up now and count the stars if you are able to, and if you can count the stars, that's how many descendants you are going to have. That's how many kids you are going to have. That's how much prosperity you are going to have. That's how much blessing you are going to have!"

"Stop looking at the ceiling above you and go out to where there are no limitations! Look at the stars and count them if you can, Abraham, and I will make your descendants like the stars of heaven."

He is saying the same thing to you and me! Anything that limits your ability to see things God's way, is the flesh.

God says “Look up!” He says, “Look out of that vertical window rather than looking out of that horizontal window at what your eye can see.” It’s not about what your eye can see. It’s about what God can see and what you can see when you walk in the spirit—and think like Him! When you do, the blessings of God will come upon you and overtake you!

About the Author

Pastor Gregory Dickow is the Founder and Senior Pastor of Life Changers International Church, one of the largest congregations in the Chicagoland area, and the Host of *Changing Your Life*, a world-wide television program reaching a potential of more than 500 million households weekly.

Now reaching around the globe, Gregory Dickow's daily and weekly television program, *Changing Your Life*, is doing just that—changing lives and empowering people to fulfill their God-given destiny. Pastor Dickow is well known for his ability to communicate the principles of God's Word in a way that people can easily understand and apply to their daily lives.

Through Gregory Dickow Ministries, hundreds of thousands of books, CD's, audio and videotapes have been distributed around the world teaching multitudes, empowering them to walk in faith, hope and God's unfailing love. Many of these powerful teachings are also printed and broadcasted on the ministry website (www.changinglives.org).

A Sample Of Other Books Available By Gregory Dickow

- Acquiring Beauty
- Breaking the Power of Inferiority
- Financial Freedom
- How to Hear the Voice of God
- How to Never Be Hurt Again
- Taking Charge of Your Emotions
- The Power to Change Anything
- Winning the Battle of the Mind

A Sample Of Audio Series Available By Gregory Dickow

- Financial Freedom: Strategies for a Blessed Life
- How to Pray & Get Results
- Love Thyself
- Mastering Your Emotions
- Redeemed from the Curse
- The Blood Covenant
- Building Your Marriage God's Way